MW00711751

Extraordinary
PARENT
A Survival Guide for
Single Parents

BY
NINA CARTER

TABLE OF CONTENTS

PART II

PART III

3

Part IV

PART VI

EXTRAORDINARY PARENT

I dedicate this book to two special people in my life, my beautiful daughters, Amia and Arianna. I love you both very much. It is such a blessing to have you in my life. I hope I make you proud.

INTRODUCTION

Oh, my goodness! I cried so hard today. Once again, I'm impatient, stressed, and tired. Raising children by myself was not my choice, but it was the hand that I was dealt. I feel so unprepared right now. How can I ever be an extraordinary parent?

It seems hopeless and impossible. I try to be nice and have patience with my children, but it lasts only a short time. I have no way of venting correctly.

I've lost me. As a single parent, I feel unhappy and insecure with myself. I struggle with understanding why life is this way for me. I need to know how to make it through and get to be the parent that I desire to be.

Have you ever felt like this? I have. In fact, I still have my less-than-stellar days. But I'm working on developing into a better parent, an extraordinary parent.

The pressures of life, in addition to the challenges of solo parenthood, can rob you of your peace of mind. This book came from my desire to connect with others who want that peace back. I want my progressing story of struggle and triumph to encourage other single parents to become extraordinary at what we do.

As you work through each day, you'll find that journaling how you feel or what you want to improve on as a parent will be helpful as you see your journey to becoming an extraordinary parent. Each day set aside time for yourself to read and journal for thirty days, implement each mission as the next day's task.

When you read back over this book after the thirty days, I want you to see what improvements you made. If you still have things you want to improve, re-read and redo until you master them. You are an extraordinary parent; together we are going to help you realize it.

PART I

The first five days deal with releasing the past, patience, purpose, attitude, and defeating limitations. These are all BIG things that we deal with as single parents.

PROGRESS

A forward or onward movement (as to an objective or to a goal).
Merriam-Webster Dictionary

It was hard for me, at one point, to get over the "past". I wanted to hang on to what was familiar; knowing that was bad for me. It really was a stronghold that I allowed to rule my life, which prevented me from moving on. I told myself one day, "I'm done, and I

13

refuse to look back". That was one of the hardest things I have ever done. When you have put your heart and time into something, it hurts to walk away. But it was hindering me from moving on and was taking my attention from the things that are really important, like my children.

I wish I could do it all over, but I can't focus on 'shoulda, coulda, woulda'. I have things to work on, like having patience with people that need it — a.k.a my children.

PATIENCE & PURPOSE

The quality of being patient, as the bearing of provocation, annoyance, misfortune, or pain, without complaint, loss of temper, irritation, or the like.

Webster Dictionary

Patience. It isn't always easy to display. It takes practice and understanding. Being a single parent can be very stressful, especially when you struggle to make a living for your family. There come times when you don't want to be bothered or you just want a nap! How do you handle that? The answer is to find your purpose.

When we clearly understand who we are and what we need to

15

do, we have to focus on that in order to complete it. It's just like college. The purpose is to obtain a degree — that's why you attend classes and do homework. We work toward these things because we have the focus to get the degree. The same goes with parenting we have a purpose and this includes being the best parent. Our children watch us and learn from us. That's why it is so important that we set an example, so they will grow up modeling behavior that is conducive to successful and extraordinary lives.

POSITIVITY

Positivity: the state or character of emphasizing what is laudable, hopeful, or to the good; constructive.

Merriam-Webster Dictionary

Oh boy, can we get some attitudes. Well, I can speak for myself at least. I have those days when I am so tired that I wish the children could take care of themselves. But guess what — they don't. Adjusting my attitude to make them understand that I am tired and not just "Mean Mommy". When I say, "Mommy's tired", that means to go play for a few minutes so that I can regroup. It can be challenging to relay this to my kids.

I'm going to tell you what doesn't work:

>Screaming at the top of your lungs. *Tried it.*
>Snapping... saying hurtful things that you shouldn't speak to your child, or any child for that matter. *Done it and not proud of it.*
>Walking away from your kids like they don't exist. *Hint: All they are going to do is follow you and keep asking.*

We have to properly communicate with our children, to help them understand that we need time alone; that Mommy or Daddy want to play the quiet game for a little bit. Children will be children, and we have to understand that. Most of us are not dealing with geniuses. So we must train our children to understand us and learn to communicate with them so that thing called a temper will eventually disappear.

LIMITATIONS

Things that set the final, utmost, or furthest boundary or point as to extent, amount, continuance, procedure, etc.
Webster's Dictionary

Single parenting means facing limitations but refusing to let them make us feel inadequate. I can think about the times when I just didn't think I was going to make it through the day. I'd come home to my daughter and thought that I was never going to be the parent that she needed. All of life's pressures made peace feel like a far away island located out of my reach. Those discouraging thoughts were feelings of limitations. We do have struggles and hardships, but nothing is too hard for God.

We've talked about purpose and how understanding our purpose is important in gaining footing for our future. That understanding also gives us the mindset to overcome barriers. We are extraordinary as single parents, individuals, sisters or brothers, friends, daughters or sons, co-workers, business owners, and just everyday living examples. You will beat these odds. I did!

You could not have told me when I was sitting in my early childhood class pregnant with my first daughter that six years later I would be a single mother of two, working on my Masters, Founder of Mirror Me Foundation, Inc., author of *Extraordinary Parent*, and happier than I have ever been in my whole life (without being in a relationship). If I can beat the odds, anyone can!

DAY ONE

Let Go of the Past

"Give thanks for what you are now, and keep fighting for what you want to be tomorrow."—Fernanda Miramontes-Landeros

What can lingering in the past accomplish? Nothing!

When you concentrate on something, you spend time on it. If it is not healthy or benefiting you in any way, take it for what it is and learn from it. Not looking back makes it easier to move on.

We are given choices and we are responsible for every one that we make. However, we can't change our past. So don't look at yesterday in a negative light. Just make sure you learned something valuable that can one day help someone else, especially your children. Even if you learned nothing from it, it still does not change the fact that it is already done. We are now where we are for a reason, whether we agree with that reason are not.

Sometimes, single parenthood proves difficult and seems unfair. On the other hand, parenting in itself can be a difficult task. You have to ask yourself how you can be a better parent. Set goals for yourself and write them down. Go at your own pace — and not anyone else's — so that you can achieve them. One day, you'll look back at what you've written and appreciate the progress you've made. As you continue to move forward, find a way to celebrate your achievements.

TODAY'S MISSION

As a single parent, I know my responsibility is great. But from this point on, I will not look at the past, but strive to reach the goals that I set for myself.

TODAY'S AFFIRMATIONS

I am an extraordinary parent.
I will achieve the goals I have for
myself.
I will not live in my past, but look
toward the future.

TODAY'S THOUGHTS

i feel like I have tried
for over 18 years to
get my kids to help
around the house and
I always face opposition.
They have no respect
for me and don't
listen no matter how
much I explain things.
I try to take things
away, and then my
parents let them

25

TODAY'S PERSONAL GOALS

do it anyway. I told
my mom again that
they can't go
anywhere if they don't
do chores and less
than an hour later
she's talking about
my 14 year old going
to her house today. I
feel like I have no
support and nothing I
do or say works or
matters to anyone,
They mess up everything I
clean and don't clean up
after themselves.

26

DAY TWO

Let Patience Guide You

"The keys to patience are acceptance and faith. Accept things as they are, and look realistically at the world around you. Have faith in yourself and in the direction you have chosen." — Ralph Marston

Stop! When everything seems to be hitting you at once, you immediately want to stop. You find yourself losing hope and question why things are the way they are. But in those times, you must remember that *"...that in all things God works for the good of those who*

27

love him (Rom. 8:28a). The word "*all*" means that nothing is excluded.

Parenting is a tough job. And doing it alone tops the cake with a big, red cherry. But if we become more patient, we will eventually succeed. *I will make it ...I will make it.* That is what you have to tell yourself, even when it looks rough.

Our job as parents is to do the best that we know how in instructing and providing for our children. That is not to say that we are perfect and will never make another mistake. We must realize that we have more challenges in parenting than the home that has both mother and father, in that we must do double duty as a parent.

But if we are called to it, we can do it.

Single parenting means sometimes putting "me" aside and making the best of what we have. As we grow in our parenting wisdom, we will increase in understanding, patience, and in our parental skills that allow us to raise our children. And we'll also continue to flourish as individuals.

TODAY'S MISSION

Today's mission: practice patience. When you would normally get upset or irritated at something today, stop and practice patience. See what other direction patience can lead you to.

29

EXTRAORDINARY PARENT

TODAY'S AFFIRMATIONS

I am an extraordinary parent.
I am patient with my children.
I may not understand, but I will be patient.
I am waiting on the full manifestation of my parental skill from God.

TODAY'S THOUGHTS

I'm jealous of other families whose kids help. I'm tired of being told it's okay for these kids to be the way they are because I was supposedly messy and a difficult teen.

TODAY'S PERSONAL GOALS

Tell my Kids patiently that they are not helping enough and be brave enough to stick with consequences if they don't. Stop letting the negative things and lack of support from my family get to me. Realize that I am not wrong for asking for respect and help from all the Kids.

DAY THREE

There is a Purpose

"I can't change the direction of the wind, but I can adjust my sails to always reach my destination." ~ Jimmy Dean

Some days, it seems like there is no purpose in what you do. Life feels like more of a routine than anything else. Each new day proves more of a challenge than the one before.

One of my favorite Bible verses reads *"...the one who is in you is greater than the one who is in the world" (1 John 4:4).*

Purpose is more of a discovery than a map to your destination. If we knew everything that would happen to us, life would be boring. Like a rehashed sitcom, it would temporarily amuse and distract us from our pre-scripted unimaginative lives.

We are who we are, and we cannot change that. What we can do is make the best of the life we have been given. If we understand that there is joy in each day that we wake up. We can start fulfilling our purpose with a little more ease and positive expectation.

In parenting, there are discouraging times, but the delightful times outweigh the discouraging ones. Discovering

33

what your purpose is will help you become a better parent. We must have direction, so our children can see some direction even though we may struggle at times.

TODAY'S MISSION

Find something that you are passionate about and see if it helps you discover a sense of purpose for your life.

TODAY'S AFFIRMATIONS

I am an extraordinary parent.
I have a purpose.
I know my purpose.
I find joy in parenting.

TODAY'S THOUGHTS

TODAY'S PERSONAL GOALS

DAY FOUR

Your attitude makes the difference

"Whenever you're in conflict with someone, there is one factor that can make the difference between damaging your relationship and deepening it. That factor is attitude." — William James

"Attitude, what attitude? I don't have an attitude". Well you may or may not have *'an attitude'*, but more likely than not, there are some adjustments that can be made when it comes to one's attitude. We may not realize it, but we have more

37

personal conflicts with issues and people than we know. When I look at myself, I notice how quickly I can get frustrated and upset at something or someone (a.k.a ATTITUDE).

Have you ever seen a child with lots of attitude in their personality and say to yourself, *"I wonder where that comes from"*? And then you get to know the parent? Believe it or not, they get it from their parent! Because we are examples to our children, our actions can become our children's own habits. That is why it is so important to have a good attitude.

Having a positive attitude helps us to be optimistic. In turn, this will help us discover all the joys that life has to offer. We may not want to have a positive attitude all the time, but it will actually help us in the long run. We will look happier, age slower, enjoy more things in life, and see improvement in our children's attitude. Having a positive attitude makes situations and issues look better, even when they are dark.

TODAY'S MISSION

Work on my attitude. I will rethink a normal reaction or interaction today, to see if the outcome will be different.

Today's Affirmations

I am an extraordinary parent.
I have a positive attitude.
I will be optimistic about issues and situations in my life.

Today's Thoughts

TODAY'S PERSONAL GOALS

DAY FIVE

Conquer your limitations

"Our limitations and success will be based, most often, on your own expectations for ourselves. What the mind dwells upon, the body acts upon."—Denis Waitley

Limitations exist. That is a known fact, but dealing with the limitations that we face is how we either defeat them or live with them. We are challenged in many areas in our lives, but it is our mission to overcome those challenges. Dealing with limitations first comes from what we think we can or cannot do. We are capable of doing just about anything. I am sure there are people that didn't think you could raise your child or children by yourself. But look. You are doing it.

This is the same way we must deal with any limitation — keep pushing forward. When you focus on what needs to be done, you defeat limitations simply by not paying attention to them. I understand that some limitations are in the forefront of our daily lives and we are consistently reminded of them, but that doesn't mean that we cannot defeat them. We conquer these limitations by embracing them and understanding how to defeat them. Once we have that understanding, we set a plan in motion. It may not happen all at once, but we can gradually work to defeat every limitation that may stand in our way. This is where patience and letting go of the past comes in.

As we defeat limitations, new limitations may arise. But we keep going because we know that we will defeat whatever challenges come our way.

TODAY'S MISSION

Take time to write down your top five biggest limitations. Then figure out three ways that you can defeat them. Make a plan and a timeline that you believe will work for you and start your defeating process today!

TODAY'S AFFIRMATIONS

I am an extraordinary parent.
I am an over comer.
I will reach all my goals.
Limitation in my life will be defeated.

TODAY'S THOUGHTS

TODAY'S PERSONAL GOALS

PART II

As parents, we deal with a lot of issues. And single parenting makes life even more difficult at times. In relationships, we have difficulty trusting someone and accepting him or her as the best person to become a part of our lives. It's not always a win-win situation, and we often give up more than we envisioned we would. And then, there are times when we have to learn from our mistakes.

Everything and everyone is not transparent in the beginning. That is why we have to always think a great deal first and take our time in getting to know someone. If we already have people in our lives that are a part of what we call *'family'*, then we must take time to make sure that welcoming this new person in is the best decision for the family as a whole. We can sometimes become selfish and not realize that the other person is not what everyone in the family needs.

Dealing with the mistakes of parenting and life choices are other issues most face. I personally had a hard time with this. I would beat myself up about the things I did wrong. But on the other hand, I began to see some good come out of the bad, and I learned from the mistakes I made. With that I also began to be more positive about my situation and how I could be proactive about the lessons I learned from these mistakes.

Another issue many of us have is comparing ourselves to others. We do it sometimes without even realizing it. Comparing ourselves to others is unhealthy. It causes us to lose focus on what we are doing because we are so busy looking at others. Each one of us is extraordinary - meaning *'extra-ordinary'*. To compare ourselves to others is like comparing apples to oranges. What is good for my family may not work for someone else's family.

Another reason comparing ourselves to others is not good is that it takes us off task. Trying to keep up with someone else keeps you from doing what you are designed to do. That is why it is so important to take the time you need to fuel yourself, physically and mentally. You need time with your family to build one another up and nourish your relationships. But you also need time for you, and your family needs time away from you. These two are important because we have a responsibility to both ourselves and our family members. If we are not meeting our own needs and care properly for our own selves, how can we do so for others, no matter how good our intentions may be?

We must understand that taking care of ourselves is okay and it is a part of the responsibilities that each

51

of us is given. If we don't, we can become disconnected from who we are as people and who our family members are as individuals. This will never benefit the family as a whole. Instead, it creates a sense of fear that we won't communicate the fundamentals that help us have a successful family.

Fear can come at many times and in many ways. Fear can come when one loses a job, when our children are not listening to us, and when family members don't understand what's going on, among other things. We often don't recognize this as fear because it disguises itself as an expected and normal part of life. But we don't have to accept any form of fear!

52

Conquering fear starts by evaluating and appreciating ourselves as individuals.

Recognizing success in ourselves will allow us to promote and pass along this positive attitude to our children. Although success is defined differently in every household, in the end it is simply to go as far as you dream. Success is doing the best that you know you can do.

DAY SIX

Dealing with relationships

"Happiness is having a dream you cannot let go of and a partner who would never ask you to."— Robert Brault

Wow, relationships can be such a touchy subject. Most of us long for positive relationships. It's part of our human nature. Whether it is a best friend or a significant other, it feels good to have people in our lives that care about us. Sometimes it does not always happen in that order and we fill like we are missing out on something. Well I'm here to tell you, there is something you can do about it.

When you feel there is a void in your life, you need to figure out where the void is and what it is. Sometimes we fill these voids with relationships and people, but they are not the real problem. Relationships can be difficult while raising children alone because they can add more pressure in your life. We sometimes try to fit people in places that need other answers. Having a mate or a person in your life that you feel secure with can mask other issues that you may have. We have to deal with these issues head on, so that when we are in a relationship, whether it be a friendship or partnership, we have a better sense of what we want.

Some may have that person in whom they feel confident in their lives. All I suggest is that you make sure they are who's best for the whole family and not just for you. If you take the time you now have and invest it in yourself, you'll have a better sense of who you are and you will be able to give yourself to the person who is really for you.

Today's Mission

Evaluate the relationships that you are in — friendships or romantic relationships .Decide if they are positive ones that do not add more stress in your life. Or do they need to be reevaluated.

TODAY'S AFFIRMATIONS

I am an extraordinary parent.
I will have positive, productive relationships in my life.
I will have a good mate.
I am worth waiting for.
I am great at evaluating issues in my life.
I am stress free.

TODAY'S THOUGHTS

TODAY'S PERSONAL GOALS

DAY SEVEN

Dealing with mistakes.

"A man's errors are his portals of discovery."— James Joyce

Mistakes are hard to deal with. We beat up on ourselves about things we did in error. This is harmful to our internal self. We must learn to deal with the mistakes we have made. When dealing with them, we have to recognize that we did something wrong. Then, we need to evaluate how we should have handled the situation and what we could do the next time it occurs.

We are not to keep the mistake in the forefront of our minds. That is dwelling on the past and it doesn't help anything. As parents, we will make mistakes. But, it is our job to trust that we learn and grow from them. On the positive side, mistakes can lead to discovery. When you realize you did something wrong or that the decision you made didn't work out for the best, you may discover a new and better way of doing something. There are things you cannot change, but there are plenty of things that you can.

TODAY'S MISSION

Deal with a mistake you made by writing it down and allowing yourself to evaluate the things that you have learned from this particular mistake. Then note how you will deal with it in a positive light.

TODAY'S AFFIRMATIONS

I am an extraordinary parent.
I am dealing with my mistakes.
My mistakes do not own me.

TODAY'S THOUGHTS

61

TODAY'S PERSONAL GOALS

DAY EIGHT

Dealing with comparing myself to others.

"You have your way. I have my way. As for the right way, the correct way, and the only way, it does not exist."— Friedrich Nietzsche

The Jones family has just returned from the Fiji Islands, and Ms. Jones comes over to tell you all about how the kids really enjoyed themselves. You take note of everything she is saying and feel bad because you have neither time nor resources to take your family on such a wonderful trip.

So you say, "Ms. Jones, I'm busy. We are going to have to finish this conversation at another time".

But when she leaves, you fall into a heavy depression. But don't you dare!

Why even compare yourself to someone else? You are responsible for your own family, and that's it. You are expected to do what you can do — not what someone else can do. No one should tell you what to do and what not to do. Understand that you can do only the best you can. If you don't have it, you just don't have it.

We must learn to not be intimidated or feel that we are not

keeping up with the rest of the world. Everyone is different, has different goals, different finances, and different households. We are not clones. We are individuals for a reason. We each have a purpose and we must understand that purpose. We must live our lives the best we know how and raise our children in the way we believe will make them motivated and successful in their lives.

TODAY'S MISSION

The mission is to not compare your family to someone else's family. We have to do what we can and understand that not everyone's views are the same.

65

Extraordinary Parent

Today's Affirmations

I am an extraordinary parent.
I do not compare my family to other families.
I will do the best that I can to raise my family.

Today's Thoughts

EXTRAORDINARY PARENT

TODAY'S PERSONAL GOALS

67

DAY NINE

Take the time you need for you

"We're so busy watching out for what's just ahead of us that we don't take time to enjoy where we are."— Calvin & Hobbes

I used to think that going away was very selfish. But now, I know that it's necessary to be the best parent I can be. When you take some time for yourself, you are able to use that time to relax, think, and create a plan. When you return to the "real world", you are refreshed and ready for your next set of challenges. It is so important to create some time that is designated to give you a chance to calmly deal with what you go through on a daily basis.

It is not always family life that makes things so stressful. There are outside forces that may escalate stress. It is okay to take a break at times. Treat yourself to something out of the ordinary. Now, I'm not saying go crazy, but I am saying that it is important to treat yourself special so you can keep your sanity.

TODAY'S MISSION

Plan to do something for yourself. Maybe a day at the spa, a weekend at the lodge, a vacation with friends, hiking, or just a weekend by yourself.

TODAY'S AFFIRMATIONS

I am an extraordinary parent.
I am happy and refreshed.
Time for myself equals a better me.
I am relaxed and will reduce stressful actions in my life.

TODAY'S THOUGHTS

70

Today's Personal Goals

DAY TEN

Do not fear

"Our deepest fear is not that we are inadequate. Our deepest fear is that we are powerful beyond measure. It is our light, not our darkness that frightens us most. We ask ourselves, 'Who am I to be brilliant, gorgeous, talented, and famous?' Actually, who are you not to be? You are a child of God. Your playing small does not serve the world.

There is nothing enlightened about shrinking so that people won't feel insecure around you. We were born to make manifest the glory of God that is within us. It's not just in some of us; it's in all of us. And when we let our own light shine, we unconsciously give other

72

people permission to do the same. As we are liberated from our own fear, our presence automatically liberates others."— Maryanne Williamson

Remember what Oprah Winfrey's character, Sophia, said in The Color Purple? "All my life I had to fight."

Wow, that's a lot of fighting! But could it be that, at times, our fighting is out of fear? Could we be in fear that if we don't fight back, we will be overtaken by all the things that come against us? Oh, how untrue!

First, God has not given us the spirit of fear. That means fear is something that comes to make you feel defeated and unable to live your life in peace. Fear is not our

73

friend because it hinders us from making steps toward progress. Sometimes we fear and don't even know it. Conquering fear is not easy. But it is possible. It just takes doing the thing that you are fearful of and hoping for the best outcome. Whatever your fear is, make sure you're aware of it and work on overcoming it. Do not fight because you have fear, but fight to conquer that fear.

TODAY'S MISSION

Write down what things you are most fearful of and list the ways you can conquer those fears.

Today's Affirmations

I am an extraordinary parent.
I will not fear.
Fear is no longer a part of my life.
I'm a conqueror, in everything I do.

Today's Thoughts

75

TODAY'S PERSONAL GOALS

PART III

You know what? Tears are not always signs of joy. They sometimes show that we care, are hurt, in pain, and many other feelings. So many times we have been taught in our society that crying is a form of weakness, but I disagree. It's okay to cry. Crying allows us to express many overwhelming feelings.

I hated crying, especially in front of other people. Now, I cry a lot — when I'm happy, disappointed, sad, upset, hurt, and the list goes on. Crying helps to relieve some of the stress and other negative energies we have inside. It's okay to cry.

Remember, God made tears for a reason.

Being happy is so important. I could write a whole book on being happy. We do not comprehend at times that we affect more than our selves when we are not happy. Our children know when we are not happy.

There was a point in my life when I was so unhappy with myself and the world. Not that things were so terrible, but I just was not happy with myself. I was not able to give my children the attention and support they needed, because I did not have the "energy". I made every excuse in the book to be alone. I did not want to be bothered. But one day, I was so tired of feeling that way. I couldn't do it anymore.

I felt the responsibility of raising my girls by myself. I mean I really felt it. It felt like too much, like I could not do it. One day, I told God I was tired and I did not want to feel this way anymore. That day, my life changed, and I have never allowed myself to go back to that place. I started to pick myself up.

I began to see that I could do this. I could handle it. I was not alone. I *did* have people who loved and supported me. I loved my girls and wanted them to have an enjoyable childhood. So I began to surround myself with the positive things that I saw every day. It was like someone began to shine a flashlight in a dark room. I realized that I have the ability to raise my girls, be successful, live my dreams, and enjoy my life. How? I decided to make the best of it all. It was not about me anymore. I had two little girls depending on me — who needed me as much as I needed them.

We are parents. We provide the love, care, and support that our children need. It is not an easy job, but we can do this. I support you because I understand your struggles. I support you, because we can do this! We will be extraordinary parents!

DAY ELEVEN

It's okay to cry.

"Tears are words the heart can't express"— Unknown

Have you ever caught yourself crying and didn't know why? Well, more than likely it is because you are so overwhelmed that the emotion you have suppressed comes out unexpectedly. It is okay to cry. Crying is a natural emotion. It is something human beings were designed to do. So no matter who told you that it is not okay, it is!

We are emotional beings and it may take us actually seeing our own tears to understand what is really going on in our lives. We sometimes make issues and problems non-existent when we really care or want to find a solution. But tears are a way of seeing how much you really care about something. Have you ever tried to cry about something and the tears just do not come? On the other hand, have you ever tried to stop crying about something and you cannot? Well, crying allows us to see how deep the emotions and feelings really are.

Single parents go through a lot of things in our lives. And though some may be self-inflicted, it still doesn't feel good when there are challenges and mistakes made. I am saying that if it takes a tear or more to get through the rough times, you have the right to cry.

TODAY'S MISSION

Today, make sure you are clear about the emotions you have experienced lately. Take the time to really discover your true feelings about the issues related to your emotions.

TODAY'S AFFIRMATIONS

I am an extraordinary parent.
I will feel free to cry.

I take time to be in touch with my emotions.

TODAY'S THOUGHTS

EXTRAORDINARY PARENT

TODAY'S PERSONAL GOALS

DAY TWELVE

Being Happy

Words to live by: "Being happy doesn't mean that everything is perfect. It means that you've decided to look beyond the imperfections."~ Unknown

Be happy? What? I am happy! Well, being happy should not be an off and on again thing. Being happy starts with appreciating yourself and living a life of happiness. This means being in touch with who you are and who you want to be.

Being a single parent does not disqualify you or disable you from

87

reaching for the sky. But it can mean that you have more challenges than the average person. However, those challenges will build character and make your success more appreciated by you and your children.

Happiness should be a part of your daily life. If you aren't happy, find out what is hindering your happiness. Being happy enhances your life and makes you a better person and parent. We have good days and bad days. But when you are genuinely happy, it doesn't make you want to go hide and not live life!

We are destined for greatness! With this attitude, you can encourage yourself to be happy. We have something to be happy about. Just look around you! Your children are why happiness should be a daily adjective in your life.

TODAY'S MISSION

Find the things that make you happy and write them down. Then evaluate if these things are what really make you happy and if you are happy without these things.

TODAY'S AFFIRMATIONS

I am an extraordinary parent.
I will be happy.
I will live in happiness.
Everything will work in my favor.

89

EXTRAORDINARY PARENT

TODAY'S THOUGHTS

TODAY'S PERSONAL GOALS

DAY THIRTEEN

You can do this

"Keep your dreams alive. Understand that to achieve anything requires faith and belief in yourself, your vision, hard work, determination, and dedication. Remember all things are possible for those who believe."— Gail Devers

Do you ever just want to scream? I do. But by the grace of God, I tell myself that I will make it.

I can look over my life and see some things that I never thought I would get through. I never thought I would accomplish my educational goals, raise my girls by myself, be okay will being single, and be happy with myself. We can do this. It is a struggle and challenge at times, but it doesn't mean that it is impossible. It is all possible! We are more than conquerors, because we believe in who we are. It may take a little extra effort, but it will be worth it all.

How many times did people, friends or family, say you couldn't do it but you did? For so many days, I didn't think I could do it. But when I think about all the things that challenged me, it gives me hope for the challenges that I am now facing.

I can do this — not because I have so much strength and power. But I am moving forward in faith.

Extraordinary Parent

When we feel like we cannot take it anymore, we must press forward. When you can look ahead, it gives you a view of what is to come, which is the victory that is on the way.

Today's Mission

Every challenge you face today, just say to yourself "I can do this".

Today's Affirmations

I am an extraordinary parent.
I can do this.
I am moving forward.
I understand my challenges and will conquer them through faith.

Today's Thoughts

TODAY'S PERSONAL GOALS

DAY FOURTEEN

Surrounding Yourself with Positivity

"And will you succeed? Yes! You will indeed! (98 and 3/4 percent guaranteed)"— Dr. Seuss

Have you ever been around someone who has a negative viewpoint on everything? Pretty soon, you begin to doubt yourself or question your decisions on the issues that you are dealing with? This comes from being around people who lack good energy and positivity.

It is important with whom you surround yourself. If you are already struggling in a certain area of your life, do not befriend someone with that same issue, or it may be very difficult for you to overcome it. We must seek out positive people that will encourage us to be better and inspire us to reach our dreams. Negativity is contagious. Remember that.

As single parents, being negative does not help us. We need to be realistic but positive about our situations. These attitudes will be what our children see and take hold of.

If it is hard to see anything positive in your life, make a list of all the good things that happened to you this week, starting with the fact that you woke up today! We cannot take the little things for granted, because the little things help push and encourage us when we don't always see the big things. I realize today, more than ever, that it is not about money, fortune, or fame. But it is about being happy and taking the time to be thankful for everything. Especially the small ones.

TODAY'S MISSION

Make a list of the things that happen to you this week you can be grateful for. Then make a list of the things you want to see happen

99

within the next week. See if it happens.

TODAY'S AFFIRMATIONS
I am an extraordinary parent.
I am grateful for all I have.
I will surround myself with positivity.
I will take time to acknowledge the little things.
I will be a positive source for others.

TODAY'S THOUGHTS

Today's Personal Goals

DAY FIFTEEN

Making the best of it all

"Everything that irritates us about others can lead us to an understanding of ourselves."— Carl Gustav Jung

Can we make the best of a bad situation? Well, of course we can. Who we are and how we view what we can accomplish comes from within. It is our job to get motivated and then make the best of it.

So, you didn't plan on life being this way? *Make the best of it.* All of your good friends are single with no children? *Make the best of it.* You don't have the income you desire? *Make the best of it.* The school keeps calling home? *Make the best of it.*

Well, you may ask, "How I can make the best of it." First, you take what you know is good and acceptable in your life, and you capitalize on it. You look at those good things and you try to make your views about them the same across the board. We have to ability to make the bad become good. But it first starts with the way we look at things. It is important that we do not let the negativity get to us but, in turn, make the best of it.

Try this quick exercise. Recall the worst thing that ever happened to you. Got it? Okay, now when it

103

first happened, I bet you thought your life was over. But the fact that you are reading this book proves that you made it through. How did you do it? You just made the best of it. And just like that, you have to make the best of every obstacle.

And remember, it's okay to cry as you make the best of things.

TODAY'S MISSION

Take a situation that is difficult for you right now and think about what you can do to change it. Write it down and place it where you will see it (refrigerator, bathroom, mirror, a wall, etc) until the situation is no longer difficult.

Today's Affirmations

I am an extraordinary parent.
I can make the best of it.
I can handle difficult situations.
I will meditate and pray about these situations.
Difficulties do not scare me, but help me become stronger.

Today's Thoughts

TODAY'S PERSONAL GOALS

PART IV

Prayer should be a part of our daily lives — not because of religious obligation — but for our spiritual needs. When you take time for yourself, you are able to take time to pray. It allows the mind to relax and concentrate on the things we do not always say out loud, our feeling about issues, and thoughts about the challenges we face. It is a part of growing and knowing who you are. It allows you to see that everything does not happen in our time, but there is a time and place for everything. It is so important to include prayer in your daily routine. It will allow you to see things that you did not see before. And it will show you that what you are doing right now is not in vain and has a purpose.

Someone may ask how I know that. Well, you have to look at the small things in life. When I would react differently to situations, I would see small changes in the behavior of my children and the people around me. For things that would normally upset me, I started using words to describe that I am upset. But I would say it with compassion. It was different. My children actually listened to what I said and family members understood me. We communicated better.

And sometimes, I would just be quiet. Silence is sometimes the unspoken answer. I am learning more that when we use silence, it prevents things from escalating. We always want to say something, to get our point across. But sometimes, it's best to just be quiet. Remember, there is a time and place for everything. When we are not quiet, we usually are not listening. It is hard to talk and listen at the same time. Not only will we hear more, but we will also teach our children the importance of listening. We are examples for our children.

"Do as I say and not as I do." Have you ever heard someone say this? Well, that is not always the case. Doing and saying should both have an importance. We are examples by what we do and what we say. It is so imperative for us parents to understand that our children are watching, even when we do not think they are. We have to be excellent examples because, sometimes, how our families view the world comes from the way we see the world and tell our children about it.

As parents, we have to know when we are overextending ourselves. We cannot save the world in one day. We have to know when we're doing too much. We do not want to do too much and still not be able to do things we desire.

111

There has to be a limit. We sometimes do not want to disappoint our children, family, or friends. But we have to do what is best for our family and us. Doing too much will lead to a lot of things, mostly negative outcomes. Yes, it is okay to push ourselves to do certain things because some things just need to be done. But we have to know the difference between what needs to be done and what can wait to be done. Remember, pace yourself!

DAY SIXTEEN

Prayer is important

"Prayer is as natural an expression of faith as breathing is of life"— Jonathan Edwards

Prayer is very much an instrumental tool of faith and for positive changes in your life. Not everyone views prayer the same, but the key is to incorporate it in your life. It will give you the results you need. Prayer is a way to release your thoughts and emotions that you seem incapable of expressing to anyone else.

113

When you pray, there are no judging faces or minds around. There's just you expressing how you feel and what you desire. Prayer is so emotionally freeing because it allows you to lay all your fears, emotions, thoughts, hope, and dreams before God with the assurance that your questions will be answered by One who can do the impossible and who is able to do exceedingly and abundantly above all we ask or think. God has a way of comforting us just through prayer. There is no better feeling because we can trust and depend on him, in every circumstance.

TODAY'S MISSION

Pray about something you've been dealing with but cannot find the answer. Really give it to God and ask him to fix it for you. See what happens.

TODAY'S AFFIRMATIONS

I am an extraordinary parent.
I will implement prayer in my daily life.
I will seek God for the things I do not understand.
I am everything I need to be.
I will not worry about it anymore.

115

TODAY'S THOUGHTS

TODAY'S PERSONAL GOALS

DAY SEVENTEEN

Know that your labor is not in vain

"Without labor nothing prospers."
— *Sophocles*

Single parenting does not come with many trophies or awards. It is a humble mission with much responsibility. If no one ever told you before that you are doing a good job, let me tell you, "You're doing a good job!"

Now, we can always do better and improve ourselves as better parents. It seems so hard at times and not everyone will understand our individual struggles, but it does not mean they do not exist. We have to know that what we are doing will not always be noticeable or found to be noteworthy with others. Being a parent is our responsibility and means that some of the things we deal with are just part of the job. On the other hand, it is a more difficult task being a single parent sometimes.

I can tell you that there have been days where I didn't think I could make it and I felt so overwhelmed. But someone came to me and said just the right words

119

that gave me hope and motivation to press on. This did not happen every time I felt low, but I am still here and I made it through the rough times.

If you are at a low point, know that you can do this and your labor is not in vain!

TODAY'S MISSION

Find something that you work really hard at and see if you can do something different. Evaluate why you work so hard in this area of your life and see if you can get some positive advice from someone that you are close to or research a positive way to make changes in

120

this area, so you do not have to spend as much time and effort in that area.

TODAY'S AFFIRMATIONS

I am an extraordinary parent.
I am doing this for a reason.
I am more than a conqueror.
I will overcome difficult times.

TODAY'S THOUGHTS

Today's Personal Goals

DAY EIGHTEEN

When to use silence

"There are times when silence has the loudest voice"— Leroy Brownlow

I am a talker, and I like to have the last word. But I am learning that silence is sometimes better than words.

Have you ever given someone that "look", and they knew just how you felt? Nonverbal communication can be very effective. It is something we must practice. When that child gets out of line, we don't always have to yell or scream, etc.

123

We have to find other ways to get the message across. Silence can offer us more peace of mind than we know.

When we get upset, not only can we negatively affect our children, but we can negatively affect our own selves. Some issues in our bodies come from overexertion and stress. Think about how much more we could save ourselves if we learned how to use more nonverbal communication. It works in public too. Has your child acted out in public, and you didn't know from where the behavior came? People are staring and the child is causing a scene but there is not much you can do, is there? Well, I've been there. But we know that with nonverbal communication, we can gently pick up the child and just communicate with them nonverbally, while rubbing their back. You know what this shows? It shows the art of patience. We are supposed to be patient and understanding. We are extraordinary, remember? Now, not everyone has this problem, but practicing silence will help in some area of our lives. I guarantee it.

Today's Mission

When there is a time today that you would normally say something, try silence and see how the situation changes.

125

TODAY'S AFFIRMATIONS

I am an extraordinary parent.
I am a good nonverbal communicator.
I will practice silence in difficult moments.

TODAY'S THOUGHTS

126

TODAY'S PERSONAL GOALS

DAY NINETEEN

Being an excellent example for your family

"What can't be done by advice can often be done by example" ~ Unknown

Being an example is not easy, especially when you are doing it by yourself. We deal with so many ups and downs that we do not realize that it can affect our parenting. How many times do we deal with challenges, disappointments, and things that upset us and still keep a positive attitude? It doesn't happen very often.

As parents, we are examples by definition. It is just a part of the job description. Being an example for our children is necessary. I did not always understand this, but it is something that life has taught me. My girls do everything that I do. And now that they are getting older, they are watching me even more closely. Being an example for them is important because what they conclude by watching me will be how they conceptualize life.

How we view life will reflect on our children. Creating a positive and productive environment is vital for our children to succeed in life. Every day may not be a great day,

129

but it should not prevent us from being positive examples for our children.

TODAY'S MISSION

Today, let's see how we can be a better example. If we are falling short in areas of our lives, make a conscious effort to change. Write it down, and implement change today. Give yourself a time frame to reach this goal.

TODAY'S AFFIRMATIONS

I am an extraordinary parent.
I am a great example.
I have a better attitude toward life.

130

Challenges and disappointments will not affect the way I lead my household.

TODAY'S THOUGHTS

TODAY'S PERSONAL GOALS

DAY TWENTY

Knowing when you're doing too much

"That which needs to be proved cannot be worth much"— Friedrich Nietzsche

Have you ever found yourself doing too much? I have, and it's not a good feeling.

As single parents, we have to be effective and proactive in what we do on a daily basis. We are responsible for so much, which can be overwhelming at times. How do we deal with it? Well, first of all you stop doing so much. We have to

133

have a priority list because it will help us discover what is most important.

We are not superheroes (*although we may often think so*). We must take care of ourselves. It is so important for us to realize when we are doing too much or else we can become accustomed to doing more than we can handle. Taking it one day at a time will help with some of the stress and exhaustion and keep us from feeling overwhelmed. We have to know how to slow down and take care of the most important things: our families.

There are many things in modern life that can bring about stress: job, significant others, school, etc. That's why it is so important that we prioritize in our lives so that we can be the best parents to our children.

TODAY'S MISSION

Create a priority list with things that you need to get done. Make sure you prioritize appropriately. Make sure you do not overwhelm yourself with too much in one day. Spread it out and see if it allows you to become more effective and productive.

135

Today's Affirmations

I am an extraordinary parent.
I am not overwhelmed by the stresses in life.
I will prioritize my daily tasks.
I will take it one day at a time.

Today's Thoughts

EXTRAORDINARY PARENT

TODAY'S PERSONAL GOALS

137

PART V

Our personal lives can be difficult to talk about at times. We are cultured to be private and to keep what happens in our family lives to ourselves. Often times, we only divulge information to people we really trust— close family members or friends. This is due to the fact that we do not want what we deal with privately to be a public conversation.

This is okay. It is a personal choice to talk about or not talk about our private business. But as a suggestion, we should talk about it. Why, someone may ask. Keeping things bottled up will only hurt us in the long run. Talking about it helps us to relive some of the emotions we may feel about certain situations. Finding someone to talk to can be difficult. The next best thing is to make sure you write it down. This way, you have a record about how you felt about the situation and when you do find someone to talk to, and it will help you see how you can grow from every situation you encounter.

Peace of mind can come from talking about issues and challenges that we deal with as parents. It is so important to have peace of mind. You are able to think more clearly and have better direction. Peace of mind comes from the willingness to let go of things that may not be good for us and understand that things will happen in due time.

We cannot rush life or be upset when things do not happen in the order that we want them to happen. Our peace of mind is important; it is a part of our excellence as a parent.

Peace of mind is not just on the inside, but it will show on the outside. You will act differently, smile more, and communicate differently. To deal with our next topic, let's talk about smiling. For me, smiling comes naturally. If I am not smiling, then there is something seriously wrong. Smiling is a gesture, and it allows you to connect with others by simply just doing it.

If we were always smiling, how would people view us? Well, more than likely, they would assume that

141

we are generally happy people. But smiling is not just for others; it is for us. Not only does it reduce wrinkles in the face, it allows us to feel better about things. Normally, when we smile we're happy, excited, etc. It has to do with something positive. But what if we smiled in not-so-positive situations? How would things change? Let's try it...

These are little things that are going to make us extraordinary. As single parents we are not going to do the typical things or have the typical reaction to adversity, we are going to be different. We are going to face our challenges head on, and we are going to win. You know how? We are going to pace ourselves.

Pacing ourselves will cause us to understand that we are not trying to just win a race, but we are trying to gain the necessary experience so that we can win every race. When you look at marathon runners, it is not about who is going the fastest. They pace themselves. That is the same with parenting. Getting everything done quick, fast, and in a hurry is not always the answer. We have to be efficient in what we do.

We say that parenting doesn't have a handbook. Well, trying to get it done really quickly will definitely not be the answer. We are challenged and we will sometimes feel like we are defeated, but we are not because the race is not given to the swift, neither is it given to the strong, but to the one that endures unto the end.

We are extraordinary, and that means we are different. We have learned that "no" does not mean never. "No" can be a challenging word, and we are equipping ourselves as single parents to become an extraordinary parent. The challenges that we face will be the stepping stones to our success because, for us, success is not an option.

DAY TWENTY-ONE

Talk about it

"Success comes from taking the initiative and following up... persisting... eloquently expressing the depth of your love. What simple action could you take today to produce a new momentum toward success in your life?"— Anthony Robbins

Talking about what we feel and think is important. When we hold things inside, we are not able to make the appropriate rationalizations that are necessary for us to be effective in our parenting. We cannot keep everything in.

Some may say that they do not have a good support system or that they do not feel comfortable in talking to others about personal issues. I have a few suggestions. There are always professionals who have been educated and trained to listen and keep what you say confidential. You know that the information you disclose to them will be kept private. These professionals can help you realize the source of issues that keep reoccurring in your life.

146

Another way to acknowledge your inner most thoughts and feelings is to write it down. Have a journal that you write in daily to relieve yourself of your mental stressors. This way, if and when these stressful events or circumstances visit you again, you can look back and remember how you overcame and successfully navigated your way through those difficult times.

TODAY'S MISSION

Talk to someone you trust about an issue you deal with and have not taken the time out to address. Allow yourself to open up to help relieve some of the stress and tension that has built up as a result of this issue.

TODAY'S AFFIRMATIONS

I am an extraordinary parent.
I will talk it out.
I will not be stressed.
I will find productive ways to solve my problems.
I am where I want to be in life.

TODAY'S THOUGHTS

TODAY'S PERSONAL GOALS

DAY TWENTY-TWO

Peace of mind

"Success is peace of mind which is a direct result of self-satisfaction in knowing you did your best to become the best you are capable of becoming."— John Wooden

Have you ever heard the saying *"A mind is a terrible thing to waste"*? Well, it is a similar waste of a life to live it without peace of mind.

As we grow to become better parents, we understand the importance of peace. You know that

150

feeling you get when the kids are loud, arguing with one another, the television is too loud, or they have every possible light and electronic device on in the house? It feels so unbearable at times that you just want to scream! Well this is the same thing we do to our minds. We overwork ourselves as we spend too much time worrying about bills, trying to get everything perfect, making dinner, running baths, combing hair, and still trying to get an adequate amount of sleep. When do we give ourselves the chance to wind down and settle our minds?

We need peace of mind in order to be effective. You can accomplish everything on your agenda, but if you don't have peace of mind, you fail your own self! We sometimes fail to realize that we are just as important as our families. If we are not healthy, we cannot provide for and ensure the health of our families. How can we be effective to others if we are not effective inwardly? It is time to take care of ourselves.

We need our children, but they really need us. In order to make sure we have longevity and effectiveness, we must have peace of mind.

TODAY'S MISSION

Write down what you think would help you achieve peace of mind. If it

152

is an action, give yourself a timeline to enact it and write down everything positive that results from it.

TODAY'S AFFIRMATIONS

I am an extraordinary parent.
I will have peace of mind.
I am healthy and prosperous.
I will have peace everywhere I go.
I am effective in my home life, work life, and daily life.

TODAY'S THOUGHTS

153

TODAY'S PERSONAL GOALS

DAY TWENTY-THREE

Your daily smiles

"A smile is a curve that sets everything straight."— Phyllis Diller

A smile can change how someone reacts to you or to a situation. It is important to smile. One good reason to smile is that it reduces lines in the face. Smiling keeps us looking younger. More importantly, smiling gives us a sense of hope. Have you ever just smiled when you were having a bad day or when things didn't go as planned? I've tried it a few times. It is not the easiest thing to do, but it does help.

Every day we should wear a smile, not only for ourselves, but for the people we affect. Have you ever heard someone say about another person, "They never smile"? And their comment always has a negative connotation to it. The lack of a smile could cause a number of things to happen. People could assume you're not happy, you're having a bad day, you're not approachable, and cause others to make many other possibly false assumptions about you.

We smile, not out of pretense or to hide what is going on, but to show that we won't allow our situations to affect how we see the world and how the world sees us. There will be times when smiling will seem like the most difficult thing in the world to do. But if we do it, we will see something change. It may change how people react to you and allow someone to say just the thing that you needed to hear, because you opened yourself up through a smile.

They say our eyes are the windows to our soul. If that is true, then our smile is the breath of life for others to capture when they have nothing else to hold on to. Remember, smiling doesn't just make things brighter for us. It makes it brighter for everyone else who sees us.

TODAY'S MISSION

Today is the day of smiles. Say hello to the people you encounter today with a smile. We will smile today because we see the positive change that is coming our way. We want to make the world a brighter place and it will start with our smiles.

TODAY'S AFFIRMATIONS

I am an extraordinary parent.
I will smile.
I am happy with who I am.

158

I know the importance of being a positive light for others with my smile.
Good things are coming my way.

TODAY'S THOUGHTS

TODAY'S PERSONAL GOALS

DAY TWENTY-FOUR

What makes you extraordinary?

"Perfection consists not in doing extraordinary things, but in doing ordinary things extraordinarily well."
— *Angelique Arnauld*

We are not extraordinary because of what others think or say about us. We are extraordinary because of how we view our own selves and how we live our daily lives.

161

If you look at the word *"extraordinary"*, it subdivides into two words *'extra'* and *'ordinary'*. We are not just ordinary. We are *'extra-ordinary'*. This means we possess the power to be more than normal or average. We have the ability to change things around us.

Some may ask what makes us extraordinary. Well, it is our ability to smile through our pain, put our children on our priority list, know where to go and how to get there, understand that our struggles are a part of our purpose, strive to be better single parents, and know that there is a plan for all of this.

So don't ever doubt yourself. Know who you are because you have the power and ability to convince others of who you are. It's like a job interview. The employer doesn't know you. But through your resume and interviewing skills, you convince them that you are just what they are looking for. You cannot go to the interview without confidence or you will never get the job!

It is the same thing as being an extraordinary parent. People may look at you and judge you, but it is your job to prove all the negative things others assume untrue. You won't do this by being an overachiever, but by understanding the areas you need work in and doing the necessary work to be a better you.

We are extraordinary, and no one can take that away from us! Believing in yourself will take you a long way and enable you to reach your destiny.

TODAY'S MISSION

Think about and write down at least five things that make you extraordinary. Now, write down how those things make you a better person, then a better parent, and finally, how those things will cause you to have a better impact upon the world.

TODAY'S AFFIRMATIONS

I am an extraordinary parent.

164

*I am limited by the definition others
have of me.*
I will reach my destiny.
I am more than a conqueror.
I live in victory.
Things will change for the best.
I believe in myself.
I know who's I am and who I am.

TODAY'S THOUGHTS

TODAY'S PERSONAL GOALS

DAY TWENTY-FIVE

Pace yourself

"If a man does not keep pace with his companions, perhaps it is because he hears a different drummer. Let him step to the music which he hears, however measured or far away.
— Henry David Thoreau

Today is today and tomorrow will be tomorrow. Guess what? There is nothing we can do to change that. But what we can learn is to take our time.

167

There was a song that I wrote, the lyrics, *"Life is but a moment, don't let it slip away. Today is not tomorrow, so please don't hesitate to take your time."* What they were saying was that sometimes, we are so worried about what tomorrow will bring that we do not take the time to enjoy today. We can only know what tomorrow has in store when tomorrow comes.

The demands of single parenting make us rush at times and we do not always take the time to enjoy what we have today. Yes, it is responsible to be prepared and to understand that tomorrow is coming. But if we are always preparing for tomorrow, when do we get to enjoy today? We need to pace ourselves. It is so important that we take what we know we need to get done, do that, and then enjoy today. We only get one *today*. Not only will rushing to get things done not help, but it will make things more stressful. If we take our time and plan for that which is necessary, we will see our daily lives shift. Then, spending time with the family will not be so difficult because we understand that cherishing the moments of *today*, will only make *tomorrow* better.

TODAY'S MISSION

Today, if you find yourself rushing and stressing about something that is not a part of today, or having

169

thoughts about things that do not affect your today, write it down and forget about it, just for today! Dwell on something positive and enjoy today. And try to spend some addition time with your family.

TODAY'S AFFIRMATIONS

I am an extraordinary parent.
I will not rush.
I will not let tomorrow's worries consume me.
I will make time for my family today.
I am living stress free.
I am happy and enjoying life, today and every day.

TODAY'S THOUGHTS

TODAY'S PERSONAL GOALS

PART VI

We have talked about writing things down throughout this book. On day 26, we will deal with the real importance of writing things down.

In our world of great technology, we have advanced in so many ways that we sometimes forget the simple things. Writing things down allows us to recall, plan, and communicate.

Yes, time may be a factor when it comes to writing. But now we have computers that allow us to document it quickly. More than anything else, writing helps us to plan effectively. It helps us to be conscious of our priority lists where we have noted our plans in order of importance. That way, we can see them, plan for them, and do them.

Just like writing things down has significance, knowing where we are going also has significance. As parents we do not always map out what is next for us or for our families. It sometimes takes a catastrophic event to actually happen before we have set a plan or direction for us and the family.

We must know where we are going. How can we expect our children to have direction if we do not have it? Though I am still young, I understand the great importance of having a plan for me and for my family. I want to educate myself so that my children will be inspired to be educated. I want to be financially stable so that I can teach my children how to save and invest properly. On the other hand, these issues cannot mean everything. I have to make room for my children to be on my priority list.

Yes, it is good to have everything in line, but it is also imperative to make sure that my children feel included, loved, and supported. They must be on my priority list. Investing and planning with and for them will be worth it. Our children are a representation of who we are. They are a lifetime investment that should most definitely be given priority.

We must remember that there will be good days and bad days, but it is all about how we handle it. As parents we face a lot of unexpected challenges and responding to them in an appropriate manner can be difficult. That is why it is so important to remember that we are human, and that everything happens for a reason. Learning from the negative can always lead to a positive outcome. Complaining does not help a negative situation. We are learning to equip ourselves to face challenges with *positive* methods.

Be proud that you are doing this because you *are* doing this. Parenting is not an easy job, and there is a greater challenge in doing it alone. We are not doing this for anyone else, but because we understand the importance of being an extraordinary parent. Our children are going to grow up (if they haven't already) and thank us for what we did and how we have influenced them, positively.

I know I am thankful for my parents and all that they have done for me. I did not always agree with what they said or did, but I am now thankful for their instructions. That is the same thing that will happen to us with our children. Maybe we know better how to communicate with one another than how we communicated with our parents. It is okay for us to be proud of what we do, because not only do we do it, but we are open to being better, learning, and taking suggestions

178

from others to be the best parents we can be.

Don't wait for someone to tell you that you are doing a great job; know that you are! We are extraordinary parents, because we are enhancing who we are to become more equipped for single parenting.

DAY TWENTY-SIX

Write it down

"You never have to change anything you got up in the middle of the night to write."
— Saul Bellow

"There is no greater agony than bearing an untold story inside you." — Maya Angelou

Some things are worth remembering, so it's a good thing that you are able to write things down in your journal. Many people

180

rely on diaries, journals, address books or records to remind themselves of the things they have done. Writing things down can help you with stress. It is difficult to remember everything, but when you have it written down, you are able to be in control of what you need to do.

Have you ever forgotten what you need to do? You get the feeling that everything is out of control and you begin to stress. Then you say to yourself, *"I should have written it down"*. I know because this happens to me a lot! That is why I use my mobile calendar, and I am also a big sticky note person. I write everything down and I find that it really helps me when it comes to

181

recalling dates and other important information.

Writing is also a form of relaxation. Taking time to journal and write down important events, will help make it easier to go back and look at things. When I was a teenager, I was very into diaries and journaling. In a recent move, I found some journals and diaries that were about 15 years old. Inside my journals were emails, letter, pictures, and all my other things that allowed me to go down memory lane. It was so refreshing! I was able to have something tangible that allowed me to take a look back. If I would not have written things down, I would not be able to do this. Writing is not for others—it is for you. Take time for you, to unwind and relax.

TODAY'S MISSION

Write down how you feel today and what you want to improve. Give yourself a goal time and when the time is up, come back and look at what you have written down. See how far you have gone and how your goals are different.

TODAY'S AFFIRMATIONS

I am an extraordinary parent.
I will write things down.
I understand the importance of written communication with myself.
I will reach my goals.

183

I have the ability to beat every challenge I have in front of me.

TODAY'S THOUGHTS

TODAY'S PERSONAL GOALS

Day Twenty-Seven

Where to go

"Forget about the consequences of failure. Failure is only a temporary change in direction to set you straight for your next success."—Denis Waitley

Have you ever felt lost; like there was a clear path and now it seems like things are so out of order? You don't know where to go or what to do? I have! This is a challenge that some of us face, and it doesn't go away overnight. We are not always going to understand why things happen the way that they do. But it is our responsibility to have a plan for how we will meet our challenges.

Knowing where to go does not always come natural. You see some people that dream about being a doctor when they were little and now, they are a doctor. On the other hand, you have people (like me) who have changed their major in college at least five times, to come out with a general studies degree. Not that there is anything wrong with that. On the outside looking in, someone may think that I didn't know where I was going, and maybe they were right. But the

187

good thing about it is that it is not important what others think; you have to have a plan for your own life. We all do not travel the same road, and that's the whole point of life. But it is very important to know where you want to go. This takes time and effort, but it is well worth it.

I would never have thought I would be in a PhD program at my age. But I had to figure out where I was going. Not just for me, but for my children. Wherever I go, I want my children to see me push for excellence. I want my example to be so great for them that the wrong decisions I made —the ones that may have negatively affected them — will be reversed. We have the ability to reverse the negative. But it will require that we choose a path of excellence. Not for the fifteen minutes of fame, but for our children and our families.

They say that single parents are at a disadvantage, and I can see why this may be true. But in our case, we are changing the negativity into something positive. We know where we want to go and we are putting it into action. Our families will be successful because we have decided to improve ourselves as single parents. We will innovate and inspire our children to achieve any dream or goal they have just by being better ourselves so we can be an example of excellence. Excellence doesn't mean perfection.

But it is surpassing ordinary standards by being extraordinary parents.

TODAY'S MISSION

Today, think of where you want to be in five, ten, and fifteen years. Write each milestone down and set goals so that you can post them somewhere you will see. As you meet each goal, cross it off and treat yourself—because you deserve it. Appreciating your efforts to meet the goals you have set will push you to meet every goal you have lined up.

TODAY'S AFFIRMATIONS

I am an extraordinary parent.
I know where I am going.
I have a plan and I will follow that plan.
I will meet every goal.
I love myself, because I am fearfully and wonderfully made.
I am successful.

TODAY'S THOUGHTS

191

TODAY'S PERSONAL GOALS

DAY TWENTY-EIGHT

Putting children on the priority list

"Making the decision to have a child is momentous. It is to decide forever to have your heart go walking around outside your body."—Elizabeth Stone

"I am so busy!" ..."I just don't have time anymore"..."I can't right now"..."Please wait, don't you see I'm doing something!"... "Don't you see I'm on the phone?"..."Go out, I'm trying to take care of this!"

193

Do these phrases sound familiar? They do to me. I'm always engulfed with something so *"important"* that my children have to wait for a response, time, and attention from me. But wait; it's not supposed to be like that. We are so busy with work, school, cleaning, bills, phone calls, and other things that sometimes, we are not putting our children on our priority list.

I can remember one day, I was on the phone. (Not an especially important conversation.) My oldest daughter came to me. She wanted me to look at something she had created with paper. I can remember telling her, "Go out of my room, I'm on the phone!" I can still see the look on her face. She was so hurt and didn't know why I couldn't just take a second to look at what she had made. That day was a wakeup call for me. I knew that I had to do something different.

Again, I am not saying that I'm perfect at it, but I have tried a lot harder to pay attention to my children. If there is a time when I am busy or doing something that is of importance, I handle it differently now. I simply tell her to please let me finish and that I will look at it when I am done. This gets a totally different response from her. We are able to communicate in a more positive manner now, and I am able to help her understand without hurting her feelings.

195

Now this may not apply to everyone, but most of us can work on spending more time with our children. It is something that I struggled with because there was a lack of communication. Now I am able to communicate in a way and spend the time with them that they need. Why or how do you ask? I put them on my priority list. No other relationship, job, school, or friendship is more important than my children. They come first, and I want them to know that. I show them that by putting them first. It is not always an easy thing to do, but in the end you will feel better and your children will grow up happier and not having to seek unnecessary attention from other people. We want our children to feel like there is no better place than home, because everything they need is there.

TODAY'S MISSION

What is on your priority list? Write down the first seven things that come to mind in the order that they come to you. Now what number did your children come in? If they are not in the first two, then you need to reevaluate your priorities.

TODAY'S AFFIRMATIONS

I am an extraordinary parent.
I will put my child(ren) on the priority list.

197

I am using my time wisely.
I am giving my child(ren) the attention they need.
I will make sure my home life is in order.

TODAY'S THOUGHTS

TODAY'S PERSONAL GOALS

DAY TWENTY-NINE

Good days, bad days ... what to do!

"The way I see it, if you want the rainbow, you gotta put up with the rain. —Dolly Parton

There will be good days and there will be bad days, but the good will always outweigh the bad. Truthfully, it seems like the bad days are too long and the good days are too short. But it is really all

200

about our prospective. We know that we will face challenges and struggles, but it is how we deal with those things that paint our outlook towards them.

What makes a *'bad day'*? It is usually when something unexpected happens that is not positive. Or it could be that we just don't have a positive outlook on that day. It is important to start every morning off with a positive attitude. No matter what we have to face, positivity will change how we deal with the situation.

Oftentimes, we find ourselves negatively reacting to the *'bad'* days we have. But what if we challenged ourselves to have the same positive attitude towards our bad days as

201

we do our good days? I know that sounds impossible, right? But, I am willing to take the challenge with you. I have declared that I will not get upset or stress myself about things I cannot change. It is my responsibility from now on to make a positive out of the negative. If we push ourselves to do things we have never done, we will find out that we are able to accomplish and overcome so much more than we ever expected. Sometimes our biggest challenge is looking past what we see and believing in what we don't see.

TODAY'S MISSION

Today, we are going to change how we think and react to negative situations. It is important to realize that we have the power to change our outlook. Write down something that made you upset, worry, feel sad or uncomfortable, etc., and write down how you can make a positive out of that situation and apply it to tomorrow.

TODAY'S AFFIRMATIONS

I am an extraordinary parent.
I am able to have a positive outlook on my situation.
I will not let my bad days control me.

203

I am ready to deal with the negative in a positive manner.
I know that my challenges will make me stronger.

TODAY'S THOUGHTS

TODAY'S PERSONAL GOALS

DAY THIRTY

Be proud of yourself as a single parent

"It's not only children who grow. Parents do too. As much as we watch to see what our children do with their lives, they are watching us to see what we do with ours. I can't tell my children to reach for the sun. All I can do is reach for it, myself. — Joyce Maynard

Often we try to explain ourselves or our situation to others. Now that I look back on how I used to view myself as a single parent, I realize that I didn't value myself much. The

206

things that I allowed to transpire in my life didn't always show that I respected and appreciated who I was as a person or as a parent.

We sometimes allow our own selves to devalue who we are, in turn causing us to make excuses for our situations. Knowing who you are as a person is the most important thing you can discover, even before becoming a parent. We do not always do this, and it then sometimes takes a mistake or wrong choice for us to be faced with the realization that we don't know who we are or what we want.

Our children watch us and will pattern their lives around the things we do. This does not mean that they will repeat everything we do. But they will grow up finding that they do a lot of things we did. In the end, we have to be happy about who we are. Yes, we may have been able to do some things differently and yes, we could have been more patient, understanding, and the list goes on. But it is our job to teach our children to be proud of who they are. The best way to do this is to be proud of who we are.

I am not perfect, but I am trying my best to be the mother that my children need in their lives. I will not point the finger at the other party. I will make up for any lack by giving my children the best. Not because I want them to favor me, but because I understand the long-term effects on my children if I do not. They did not ask to be here, and if I take the easy way out too, what kind of example am I? I chose to be proud of myself not just to teach them by example, but for me. Before I can genuinely love someone else, even my children, I have to love myself first. It has been a long struggle for me to believe in me. And I am still a work in progress. But I'll tell you one thing, I know myself better now than I ever have. I respect who I am, more than I ever have. I am comfortable in my own skin, and I love it.

It takes a strong person to do what we do every day, and it is okay to be proud of who you are and what you are doing for your children. When you make it look easy, you are doing something right.

We are extraordinary parents not just for who we are, but because of what we do. It's more than okay to be proud of that.

TODAY'S MISSION

Write a list of things you can be proud of for accomplishing. Then ask your loved ones and children what accomplishments you have made that they are proud of. See if they are the same or if they add to your list. You will be surprised to know what others consider accomplishments, we make not even recognize.

TODAY'S AFFIRMATIONS

I am an extraordinary parent.
I am proud of who I am.
I will not talk down on my situations.
I will not compare myself to anyone.
I am who I am, because I am who I am.
I will take time for me.
I love myself.
I am fearfully and wonderfully made.

TODAY'S THOUGHTS

211

TODAY'S PERSONAL GOALS

ABOUT THE AUTHOR

Small-town girl.
Pastor's kid.
Nineteen.
Pregnant.
Scared.

If you would have told Nina Carter that six years later she would have a Master's degree, a thriving program for teen girls (Mirror Me Foundation, Inc.), author of a book *Extraordinary Parent,* and be enrolled in a doctorate program...she would hardly believe you.

213

Today, the Fort Wayne native is happier than ever. Her noodles may overcook and laundry may shrink. But she's more interested in raising great kids who have solid values and integrity.

Nina encourages others in knowing that overcoming the unique challenges of solo parenting is more than possible.

If she can beat the odds, anyone can.

Write the Author:

Nina Carter
P.O. Box 10172
Fort Wayne, IN 46850-0172
Nmcprofessional85@yahoo.com

EXTRAORDINARY PARENT

A Survival Guide for Single Parents

This book is a 30-day inspirational guide for single parenting. While thirty days may not seem like a long time, if you can master these issues and challenges, your mastery can become a solid habit in thirty days.

Once you understand these basic steps you can apply them to your daily personal life. It starts with us, parents. We have to understand that our children are a product of our parenting. Parenting isn't easy or trouble-free, but learning how to deal with expected and unexpected problems will allow us to become better parents.

Join me on this thirty-day journey in learning how to become a better and less stressed single parent.

CPSIA information can be obtained
at www.ICGtesting.com
Printed in the USA
FSHW011634290220
67522FS